The Authority and Responsibilities of the Mayor of Toronto

by Matti Charlton

In plain language, this document details the role of the Mayor of Toronto, their authority and their responsibilities.

Contents

1

Introduction

The introduction section provides a comprehensive understanding of the role of the Mayor in Toronto and offers an overview of their authority and responsibilities. It serves as a foundation for understanding the significance of the Mayor's position within the municipal government and their impact on the city's governance.

Explanation of the role of the Mayor in Toronto

The role of the Mayor in Toronto is a position of significant leadership and responsibility. The Mayor serves as the highest-ranking official in the municipal government, representing the city and its residents. They are elected by the public to fulfill various duties and play a pivotal role in decision-making processes that shape the city's policies, initiatives, and overall development.

As the Mayor, they are entrusted with upholding the interests of the city and its residents, working towards the betterment of Toronto's communities and addressing the diverse needs and priorities of its population. The Mayor's role encompasses a wide range of responsibilities that span policy development, governance, community engagement, financial management, and more.

Overview of the authority and responsibilities

The Mayor of Toronto holds significant authority within the municipal government. They act as the chief executive officer of the city, providing leadership and guidance to various departments and agencies. Their executive authority allows them to appoint and remove key officials, ensuring the effective functioning of the city administration and staff.

Additionally, the Mayor has legislative authority, presiding over City Council meetings and casting a deciding vote in the event of a tie. They have the power to veto or approve decisions made by the City Council, influencing the direction and outcomes of various policies and bylaws.

The Mayor's authority extends to emergency powers as well. In times of crisis or emergencies, they have the ability to declare emergencies, mobilize resources, and coordinate response efforts. This authority is crucial for ensuring the city's preparedness, safety, and effective management of unexpected situations.

Moving beyond authority, the Mayor of Toronto carries a wide range of responsibilities. These responsibilities include policy development and implementation, where they set the city's strategic direction, develop and implement policies and programs, and ensure that these policies align with the needs and priorities of the community.

The Mayor also takes on the responsibility of planning and development, overseeing land use planning and zoning decisions, approving major development projects, and promoting sustainable urban development and infrastructure.

Other responsibilities of the Mayor include ensuring the delivery of essential services, such as transportation, water, and waste management, and supporting community initiatives and programs that contribute to the overall well-being of Toronto's residents.

The Mayor plays a significant role in economic development and job creation, attracting investments, supporting local businesses and entrepreneurs, and promoting job opportunities and workforce development within the city. Financial management is another key responsibility, with the Mayor involved in developing and presenting the city budget, ensuring fiscal responsibility, and effectively managing the city's finances and resources.

The Mayor also serves as a representative of the city, engaging with the public, building partnerships, and advocating for Toronto's interests at regional and international levels. They act as the official spokesperson for the city, attending public events, conferences, and meetings on behalf of Toronto.

2

Authority

The authority of the Mayor of Toronto encompasses several key aspects that define their role within the municipal government and contribute to their overall effectiveness in leadership and decision-making.

Chief Executive of the City

The Mayor of Toronto holds the significant authority of serving as the chief executive of the city. This position grants them executive powers to oversee and manage the day-to-day operations of the municipal government. As the chief executive, the Mayor provides leadership and direction to various departments and agencies, ensuring the effective implementation of policies, programs, and services.

The Mayor's executive authority enables them to make strategic decisions and set the overall direction for the city's governance. They work closely with city administrators, senior officials, and department heads to develop and execute initiatives that align with the priorities and vision of Toronto.

As the chief executive, the Mayor also plays a vital role in managing the city's administrative functions. They have the power to appoint and remove key officials, including the city manager and other senior positions, ensuring that the administration operates efficiently and effectively. By appointing capable individuals to leadership positions, the Mayor helps shape the organizational structure and culture of the municipal government.

Additionally, the Mayor is responsible for overseeing the implementation and enforcement of city bylaws, regulations, and policies. They collaborate with relevant departments and agencies to ensure compliance and address any issues that may arise. This authority allows the Mayor to maintain order, uphold the rule of law, and protect the best interests of the city and its residents.

In summary, as the chief executive of the city, the Mayor holds significant authority in managing and leading the municipal government. They provide direction, make strategic decisions, and oversee the day-to-day operations. The Mayor's executive powers include appointing key officials, managing administrative functions, and ensuring the enforcement of city bylaws and regulations. Through their leadership and executive authority, the Mayor plays a crucial role in driving the effective and efficient functioning of Toronto's government to serve the needs of the community.

Head of the Municipal Government

The Mayor of Toronto serves as the head of the municipal government, playing a central role in shaping the governance and policy-making processes of the city. As the head of the government, the Mayor holds significant authority and responsibility in ensuring the smooth functioning of the municipality.

The Mayor's role as the head of the municipal government involves presiding over City Council meetings, which are the primary decision-making bodies for the city. They lead these meetings, setting the agenda, moderating discussions, and casting a vote when necessary. The Mayor's leadership in these meetings is crucial for facilitating productive discussions, reaching consensus, and making informed decisions on matters that impact the city and its residents.

In addition to presiding over City Council meetings, the Mayor also has the power to veto or approve decisions made by the Council. This authority allows the Mayor to influence the direction and outcomes of various policies, bylaws, and initiatives. By exercising this power, the Mayor ensures that the decisions align with the best interests of the city and its residents.

Furthermore, the Mayor's role as the head of the municipal government involves collaborating with City Council members to develop and implement policies that address the needs and priorities of Toronto. The Mayor works closely with Council members, seeking their input and building consensus to promote effective governance and decision-making.

The Mayor also represents the city in intergovernmental relations, engaging with provincial and federal authorities to advocate for Toronto's interests. They play a crucial role in building partnerships and fostering positive relationships with other levels of government, working towards shared goals and securing resources and support for the city.

As the head of the municipal government, the Mayor acts as a unifying force, bringing together diverse stakeholders, community groups, and organizations to work towards common objectives. They promote collaboration, dialogue, and engagement, fostering a sense of unity and collective responsibility in addressing the challenges and opportunities facing the city.

In summary, as the head of the municipal government, the Mayor holds significant authority and responsibility in shaping the governance and policy-making processes of Toronto. They preside over City Council meetings, cast votes, and have the power to veto or approve decisions. The Mayor collaborates with Council members, engages in intergovernmental relations, and represents the city in various capacities. By exercising their authority and leadership, the Mayor plays a crucial role in promoting effective governance, decision-making, and collaboration within the municipal government for the betterment of Toronto and its residents.

3

Responsibilities

The responsibilities of the Mayor of Toronto are diverse and wide-ranging, encompassing various aspects of governance, community engagement, financial management, and leadership. These responsibilities highlight the Mayor's role as a key figure in shaping the city's policies, representing the community, and ensuring effective administration.

Policy and Decision-Making

Setting the Agenda for City Council Meetings

One of the key responsibilities of the Mayor of Toronto is setting the agenda for City Council meetings. This crucial task involves determining the topics and issues that will be discussed during the Council sessions. The Mayor, in collaboration with City Council members and city administrators, identifies the pressing matters that require attention, ensuring that the Council's time is used efficiently and effectively.

Setting the agenda requires careful consideration of the needs and priorities of the city, as well as the concerns and interests of its residents. The Mayor plays a vital role in ensuring that a diverse range of topics is included, encompassing matters of public importance, policy development, community concerns, and ongoing projects. By setting the agenda, the Mayor shapes the direction and focus of City Council meetings, ensuring that important matters are addressed and discussed.

The Mayor's responsibility in setting the agenda involves balancing the need for timely decision-making with the necessity for thorough deliberation. They work closely with City Council members to gather input and feedback on potential agenda items, taking into account the various perspectives and priorities of the Council. The Mayor's goal is to foster a collaborative and inclusive decision-making process that reflects the interests and aspirations of the community.

Additionally, the Mayor considers the broader strategic goals and vision for the city when setting the agenda. They may prioritize issues related to sustainable development, economic growth, social equity, infrastructure improvement, or other key areas that contribute to the overall well-being of Toronto. The agenda-setting process is an opportunity for the Mayor to demonstrate leadership and provide a clear direction for City Council in addressing the challenges and opportunities facing the city.

Furthermore, the Mayor ensures that the agenda is transparent and accessible to the public. By publishing the agenda in advance and making it available to the community, the Mayor promotes openness and encourages public participation in the decision-making process. This allows residents to be informed about the topics to be discussed and provides them with an opportunity to engage with their elected representatives on matters of importance.

In summary, setting the agenda for City Council meetings is a significant responsibility of the Mayor. It involves careful consideration of the city's needs, collaboration with City Council members, and a commitment to transparency and public engagement. By setting the agenda, the Mayor ensures that the Council's time is used effectively and that important issues are addressed, contributing to the overall governance and decision-making process in Toronto.

Leading and Chairing City Council Meetings

Another important responsibility of the Mayor of Toronto is to lead and chair City Council meetings. As the presiding officer, the Mayor plays a crucial role in ensuring that the meetings are conducted in an orderly and efficient manner, fostering productive discussions and facilitating decision-making.

Leading City Council meetings involves setting the tone and creating an environment conducive to open dialogue and respectful debate. The Mayor establishes and enforces the rules of procedure, ensuring that all participants adhere to established protocols and that discussions are conducted in a fair and transparent manner. By providing effective leadership, the Mayor encourages City Council members to express their opinions, engage in constructive dialogue, and contribute to the decision-making process.

In their role as the meeting chair, the Mayor guides the flow of discussions, ensuring that all agenda items are addressed, and that adequate time is allocated for meaningful deliberation. They have the responsibility to recognize Council members who wish to speak, manage speaking time limits, and encourage balanced participation from all members. The Mayor's leadership in chairing the meetings helps to maintain order, manage conflicts, and promote an atmosphere of collaboration and mutual respect.

The Mayor's presence as the meeting chairperson signifies their commitment to upholding the principles of democratic governance and ensuring fair representation of diverse viewpoints. They impartially moderate debates, ensure that all perspectives are heard, and facilitate the decision-making process. The Mayor may also provide guidance on procedural matters, clarify points of discussion, and help Council members navigate complex issues.

As the chair, the Mayor holds the authority to make rulings on points of order and procedural matters. They are responsible for interpreting and applying the rules of procedure, making determinations when conflicts arise, and ensuring that the meetings adhere to established guidelines. The Mayor's fair and consistent application of these rules fosters an atmosphere of fairness and impartiality.

Effective leadership and chairing of City Council meetings require the Mayor to possess strong communication and interpersonal skills. They must be able to navigate diverse opinions, manage conflicting interests, and guide the Council towards consensus and informed decision-making. The Mayor's ability to foster collaboration and maintain the integrity of the decision-making process contributes to the overall effectiveness of City Council in addressing the needs and concerns of the community.

In conclusion, leading and chairing City Council meetings is a significant responsibility of the Mayor. It requires effective leadership, impartiality, and a commitment to fair and transparent decision-making. By guiding discussions, ensuring adherence to established procedures, and promoting respectful dialogue, the Mayor plays a vital role in facilitating productive City Council meetings that contribute to the governance and development of Toronto.

Voting on bylaws and policies

The Mayor of Toronto, as a member of City Council, has the important responsibility of voting on bylaws and policies that shape the governance and direction of the city. This role involves actively participating in the decision-making process, considering the best interests of Toronto and its residents when casting votes.

Voting on bylaws and policies requires careful review and analysis of proposed measures. The Mayor must thoroughly examine the details of each bylaw or policy, considering its potential impact on the community, alignment with strategic goals, and compliance with legal and regulatory requirements. The Mayor may consult with experts, city administrators, and constituents to gather additional insights and perspectives before making an informed decision.

The Mayor's vote holds significant weight in determining the outcomes of key decisions. They have the opportunity to influence the direction of policies and bylaws, ensuring that they reflect the priorities and values of Toronto. The Mayor's vote carries the responsibility of considering the diverse needs of the city's population, balancing competing interests, and making decisions that promote the overall well-being and progress of Toronto.

In addition to individual votes, the Mayor may also play a role in building consensus among City Council members. They have the responsibility to engage in discussions, seek common ground, and facilitate collaborative decision-making. The Mayor's leadership and persuasive abilities can help bridge differences and encourage Council members to find shared solutions, leading to more effective and inclusive outcomes.

It is important for the Mayor to demonstrate transparency and accountability in their voting decisions. They should clearly communicate their rationale for supporting or opposing specific bylaws and policies, providing justifications that are grounded in the best interests of the city and its residents. This helps foster public trust and understanding of the decision-making process, ensuring that the community is informed about the factors considered in shaping the city's policies.

The Mayor's role in voting on bylaws and policies extends beyond individual decisions. They contribute to the development of a comprehensive and coherent policy framework for the city, working collaboratively with City Council members to align initiatives, address emerging challenges, and seize opportunities for growth and development. The Mayor's votes, in conjunction with those of other Council members, shape the collective decisions that guide Toronto's progress.

In summary, voting on bylaws and policies is a significant responsibility of the Mayor. It requires careful analysis, consideration of community needs, and a commitment to transparency and accountability. By actively participating in the decision-making process and casting informed votes, the Mayor contributes to shaping the policies and governance of Toronto in a manner that reflects the best interests of the city and its residents.

Proposing and advocating for new policies and initiatives

As the leader of Toronto, the Mayor has a crucial responsibility to propose and advocate for new policies and initiatives that promote the welfare and progress of the city. This role involves identifying emerging issues, envisioning innovative solutions, and championing policies that address the evolving needs and aspirations of Toronto's residents.

Proposing new policies and initiatives requires a comprehensive understanding of the challenges and opportunities facing the city. The Mayor must stay informed about local, national, and global trends, engage with community members, experts, and stakeholders, and conduct research to develop evidence-based proposals. They must identify gaps in existing policies, areas where improvement is needed, and novel approaches that can enhance the quality of life in Toronto.

The Mayor's proposals serve as a catalyst for change and progress in the city. They may include initiatives related to public safety, affordable housing, transportation, economic development, environmental sustainability, social inclusion, or other areas of importance. These proposals are informed by the Mayor's vision for the city and the priorities identified through extensive consultation with constituents and key stakeholders.

In addition to proposing new policies, the Mayor plays a critical role in advocating for their adoption and implementation. They act as a vocal advocate for the proposed policies, engaging with City Council members, community leaders, and the public to build support and consensus. The Mayor employs effective communication strategies, such as public speeches, media appearances, and community engagement events, to convey the rationale, benefits, and potential impact of the proposed policies.

The Mayor's advocacy efforts extend beyond the city itself. They may engage in intergovernmental relations, lobbying provincial or federal authorities, and collaborating with other municipalities to advance shared policy objectives. By leveraging their position and influence, the Mayor seeks to garner support, resources, and partnerships to facilitate the successful implementation of proposed policies and initiatives.

It is essential for the Mayor to demonstrate leadership and persuasion skills when proposing and advocating for new policies. They must effectively communicate the intended outcomes, anticipate potential challenges, and address concerns raised by stakeholders. The Mayor actively seeks input from City Council members, community organizations, and residents, recognizing the value of diverse perspectives and fostering a sense of ownership among stakeholders.

The proposal and advocacy process also involve collaboration with City Council members. The Mayor works closely with Council members to build consensus, solicit feedback, and incorporate diverse viewpoints into the policy development process. By fostering collaboration and shared decision-making, the Mayor ensures that proposed policies and initiatives reflect the collective aspirations of the city's elected representatives.

In summary, proposing and advocating for new policies and initiatives is a significant responsibility of the Mayor. It requires a deep understanding of the city's needs, the ability to envision innovative solutions, and effective communication and persuasion skills. By proposing policies that address emerging challenges, championing their adoption, and collaborating with stakeholders, the Mayor plays a vital role in shaping the direction and progress of Toronto, ultimately working towards the betterment of the city and the well-being of its residents.

Representing the City

Acting as the official spokesperson for the city

One of the primary responsibilities of the Mayor of Toronto is to serve as the official spokesperson for the city. In this role, the Mayor represents the collective voice and interests of the city and acts as a public face for Toronto's government and its residents.

As the official spokesperson, the Mayor communicates the city's positions, policies, and initiatives to the public, media, and various stakeholders. They have the responsibility to articulate the city's vision, goals, and priorities, ensuring that accurate and consistent messaging is conveyed. The Mayor must stay well-informed about key issues and developments within the city, as well as the broader political and social landscape, in order to effectively communicate the city's stance on important matters.

The Mayor's role as the official spokesperson involves delivering public speeches, participating in press conferences, and engaging with the media to provide updates and address inquiries. They must effectively convey complex information in a clear and concise manner, making it accessible to a wide range of audiences. The Mayor's communication skills, including their ability to connect with diverse communities, foster trust, and inspire confidence, are essential in representing the city effectively.

Acting as the official spokesperson requires the Mayor to be adept at managing public relations and handling crisis situations. They must be prepared to address controversies, respond to public concerns, and navigate challenging issues with tact and diplomacy. The Mayor's ability to communicate transparently, address public inquiries, and provide timely and accurate information fosters public trust in the city's leadership.

The Mayor's role as the official spokesperson also extends to engaging with external stakeholders, including other levels of government, community organizations, business leaders, and international counterparts. They represent Toronto's interests in intergovernmental discussions, negotiations, and collaborations, advocating for the city's needs and priorities. The Mayor's effective representation enhances Toronto's reputation, strengthens partnerships, and fosters cooperation for the betterment of the city.

In addition to external communications, the Mayor plays a crucial role in engaging with residents and communities within the city. They actively listen to the concerns, aspirations, and feedback of the public, ensuring that their perspectives are considered in decision-making processes. The Mayor's ability to connect with diverse communities, build relationships, and address local issues helps foster a sense of inclusivity and promotes civic participation.

The Mayor's role as the official spokesperson demands a strong commitment to transparency, accountability, and ethical conduct. They must uphold the highest standards of integrity in their public communications, ensuring that the city's interests are prioritized over personal or political considerations. The Mayor's professionalism and adherence to ethical principles contribute to maintaining public confidence in the city's leadership.

In summary, acting as the official spokesperson for the city is a significant responsibility of the Mayor. It requires effective communication skills, a deep understanding of the city's issues, and the ability to represent Toronto's interests at various levels. By articulating the city's positions, engaging with the media and stakeholders, and fostering public trust, the Mayor plays a vital role in shaping the city's image, promoting transparency, and ensuring effective communication between the government and its constituents.

Representing the city in intergovernmental relations

Another important responsibility of the Mayor of Toronto is to represent the city in intergovernmental relations. This involves engaging with various levels of government, including provincial, federal, and international counterparts, to advocate for the city's interests, collaborate on shared priorities, and seek support for key initiatives.

As the representative of the city, the Mayor plays a crucial role in building relationships and partnerships with other governments. They participate in meetings, conferences, and forums where intergovernmental discussions take place, ensuring that Toronto's voice is heard and its concerns are addressed. The Mayor works closely with City Council, city staff, and relevant stakeholders to identify areas of mutual interest, align policy goals, and pursue collaborative opportunities.

In intergovernmental relations, the Mayor acts as an advocate for Toronto, conveying the city's unique needs, challenges, and aspirations. They present compelling arguments and evidence to support Toronto's position on important issues, seeking alignment and cooperation from other levels of government. The Mayor must effectively communicate the city's priorities and their implications for Toronto's residents, emphasizing the potential benefits of collaborative action.

Through intergovernmental relations, the Mayor seeks to secure funding, resources, and support for critical projects and initiatives that contribute to the city's growth and well-being. This may include seeking financial assistance for infrastructure development, affordable housing initiatives, public transportation improvements, or investments in education and healthcare. The Mayor's ability to negotiate, build consensus, and advocate persuasively helps advance Toronto's interests and secure necessary resources for the city.

The Mayor's engagement in intergovernmental relations extends beyond seeking financial support. They collaborate with other governments to address shared challenges, such as climate change, economic development, public safety, and social issues. The Mayor actively participates in discussions and policy-making processes related to these areas, contributing Toronto's perspectives, experiences, and expertise. By forging partnerships and seeking common ground, the Mayor helps drive meaningful change and promote the well-being of Toronto's residents.

In addition to formal intergovernmental forums, the Mayor also engages in informal networking and relationship-building activities. This may involve attending events, meetings, and conferences where interactions with other political leaders and decision-makers occur. These opportunities provide a platform for the Mayor to establish personal connections, deepen relationships, and strengthen Toronto's influence in broader political circles.

The Mayor's role in representing the city in intergovernmental relations requires diplomacy, strategic thinking, and a deep understanding of political dynamics. They must navigate complex political landscapes, understand the interests and priorities of other governments, and find common ground to achieve mutually beneficial outcomes. The Mayor's ability to collaborate, negotiate, and build consensus contributes to successful intergovernmental relations and the advancement of Toronto's interests.

Ultimately, by effectively representing the city in intergovernmental relations, the Mayor plays a vital role in advancing Toronto's position on the regional, national, and international stage. Their advocacy, relationship-building, and collaborative efforts contribute to securing resources, addressing shared challenges, and promoting Toronto's well-being and prosperity.

Attending public events, conferences, and meetings on behalf of the city

Another important responsibility of the Mayor of Toronto is to attend public events, conferences, and meetings on behalf of the city. This includes a wide range of engagements, such as community gatherings, cultural celebrations, business conferences, and international summits. By actively participating in these events, the Mayor represents the city, engages with diverse stakeholders, and promotes Toronto's interests.

Attending public events allows the Mayor to connect with residents, community organizations, and various interest groups within the city. It provides an opportunity to listen to the concerns and aspirations of the public, understand the needs of different communities, and demonstrate the city's commitment to inclusivity and civic engagement. The Mayor's presence at these events fosters a sense of community, promotes dialogue, and strengthens relationships with the city's diverse population.

Additionally, the Mayor's participation in conferences and meetings, both locally and internationally, is crucial for showcasing Toronto's strengths, sharing best practices, and staying informed about emerging trends and innovations. These gatherings provide a platform for the Mayor to engage with other political leaders, experts, and stakeholders, exchanging ideas, building partnerships, and advancing Toronto's interests.

When attending public events, conferences, and meetings, the Mayor represents the city's official positions and initiatives. They deliver speeches, participate in panel discussions, and engage in networking opportunities to communicate Toronto's achievements, challenges, and future plans. The Mayor's role is to effectively articulate the city's vision, highlight its accomplishments, and advocate for the resources and support needed for continued growth and success.

By attending these events, the Mayor also serves as an ambassador for Toronto, promoting the city's reputation, attracting investments, and fostering collaboration. They showcase Toronto's economic potential, cultural diversity, and vibrant community spirit to local, national, and international audiences. The Mayor's active involvement in these engagements helps enhance Toronto's profile, positioning the city as a desirable destination for business, tourism, and talent.

In addition to representing the city, attending public events, conferences, and meetings also provides the Mayor with valuable opportunities for learning and sharing knowledge. They can gain insights from experts, engage in discussions on pressing issues, and bring back innovative ideas and approaches that can benefit Toronto. The Mayor's active participation in these forums ensures that they remain well-informed about emerging trends, challenges, and opportunities relevant to the city.

Attending public events, conferences, and meetings requires the Mayor to manage a demanding schedule, balancing numerous commitments and engagements. It demands strong organizational skills, the ability to prioritize effectively, and the capacity to adapt to various settings and audiences. The Mayor's presence and active participation in these events demonstrate their dedication to serving the city and their commitment to engaging with the public and other stakeholders.

In summary, attending public events, conferences, and meetings on behalf of the city is an essential responsibility of the Mayor. It provides a platform for connecting with the community, engaging with stakeholders, showcasing Toronto's strengths, and advocating for the city's interests. Through active participation in these engagements, the Mayor contributes to fostering a sense of community, promoting Toronto's reputation, and advancing the city's goals and aspirations.

Budget and financial management

Preparing and presenting the annual city budget

One of the key responsibilities of the Mayor of Toronto is to prepare and present the annual city budget. This critical task involves assessing the city's financial needs, setting budgetary priorities, and allocating resources to various departments and programs.

The process begins with the Mayor working closely with city staff, including finance professionals and department heads, to gather information about the city's financial status, revenue projections, and expenditure requirements. This involves analyzing financial data, reviewing departmental budget requests, and identifying areas that require additional funding or cost-saving measures.

The Mayor then leads the development of a comprehensive budget proposal that addresses the city's strategic objectives, responds to the needs of the community, and ensures fiscal responsibility. This includes formulating budgetary policies, making difficult decisions about resource allocation, and considering input from City Council, community stakeholders, and the public.

The budget proposal incorporates various components, including operating expenses, capital investments, and reserves. It outlines the funding priorities for key areas such as infrastructure, public services, social programs, public safety, and economic development. The Mayor must balance competing demands, evaluate the potential impact of budgetary decisions, and strive to maximize the benefits for Toronto's residents and businesses.

Once the budget proposal is finalized, the Mayor presents it to City Council for review and approval. This involves delivering a comprehensive budget speech that outlines the priorities, rationale, and key components of the proposed budget. The Mayor must effectively communicate the budget's impact on the city and its residents, addressing concerns and seeking support from Council members and the public.

During the budget review process, the Mayor collaborates with City Council to evaluate the proposed allocations, address concerns, and seek input from Council members. This may involve participating in budget committee meetings, engaging in discussions with Councilors, and considering amendments to the budget proposal based on feedback and deliberations. The Mayor's leadership and ability to build consensus play a crucial role in shaping the final budget that reflects the collective decisions of City Council.

Following the approval of the budget by City Council, the Mayor is responsible for overseeing its implementation. This includes monitoring the execution of the budget, ensuring adherence to financial plans, and addressing any unforeseen challenges or adjustments that may arise during the fiscal year. The Mayor works closely with the city's finance department to track financial performance, assess the effectiveness of budgetary decisions, and make necessary adjustments to maintain fiscal stability.

Preparing and presenting the annual city budget requires a strong understanding of financial management principles, the ability to analyze complex financial data, and the capacity to make informed decisions that align with the city's strategic goals. The Mayor's leadership in this process ensures that the city's resources are allocated efficiently, priorities are addressed, and fiscal accountability is maintained.

By actively engaging in the budgeting process, the Mayor plays a vital role in shaping the financial future of Toronto. Through careful assessment, strategic planning, and effective communication, the Mayor ensures that the city's financial resources are allocated in a manner that supports the well-being and development of the community, promotes sustainable growth, and addresses the evolving needs of Toronto's residents and businesses.

Working with City Council to approve the budget

Another crucial responsibility of the Mayor of Toronto is to work collaboratively with City Council to approve the budget. While the Mayor plays a central role in preparing and presenting the annual city budget, the final approval rests with City Council, requiring effective communication, negotiation, and consensus-building.

The Mayor engages with City Council members throughout the budget process, providing regular updates, sharing information, and seeking their input and feedback. This collaborative approach ensures that Councilors are well-informed about the budget proposals, understand the financial implications, and have an opportunity to influence budgetary decisions.

As the budget proposal is presented to City Council, the Mayor delivers a comprehensive budget speech, highlighting the key components, priorities, and rationale behind the proposed allocations. The Mayor's role is to effectively communicate the budget's impact on the city and its residents, fostering transparency and facilitating an open and constructive dialogue among Council members.

Following the budget presentation, City Council conducts a thorough review of the proposed budget. The Mayor actively participates in budget committee meetings, engaging in discussions, addressing questions, and providing additional context and justification for specific budgetary decisions. The Mayor's presence and expertise contribute to informed deliberations and enable Councilors to make well-informed decisions.

During the budget review process, the Mayor listens to Councilors' concerns, suggestions, and proposed amendments to the budget. They consider these inputs and work collaboratively to find common ground and reach consensus on budgetary matters. This may involve engaging in negotiations, exploring alternative options, and finding compromises that balance competing priorities and ensure the best interests of the city and its residents.

The Mayor's leadership skills play a vital role in guiding Councilors through the budget approval process. They facilitate discussions, foster constructive debate, and encourage Council members to voice their perspectives and advocate for their respective constituents. The Mayor's ability to build consensus and navigate differing opinions helps City Council reach a collective decision on the final budget.

Once City Council has reviewed, debated, and made necessary amendments to the proposed budget, they vote on its approval. The Mayor, as the presiding officer of Council meetings, oversees the budget approval process, ensuring that all Councilors have the opportunity to express their views and vote on the budget. The Mayor's role is to maintain order, follow procedural rules, and ensure a fair and transparent decision-making process.

Upon the successful approval of the budget by City Council, the Mayor works closely with the city's administration and finance department to implement the approved budget. This involves monitoring the execution of the budget, ensuring that the allocated funds are utilized in accordance with the approved plans, and addressing any challenges or adjustments that may arise during the fiscal year.

Working with City Council to approve the budget requires strong leadership, effective communication, and the ability to navigate diverse opinions and priorities. The Mayor's collaborative approach fosters a sense of shared responsibility and ensures that the budget decisions reflect the collective decisions of City Council, balancing the needs and aspirations of the community.

By actively engaging with City Council in the budget approval process, the Mayor demonstrates their commitment to democratic decision-making, accountability, and transparency. The Mayor's collaborative efforts contribute to a balanced and responsible budget that aligns with the strategic goals of the city, addresses the needs of the community, and reflects the collective aspirations of City Council and the residents of Toronto.

Overseeing financial management and ensuring fiscal responsibility

The Mayor of Toronto holds the important responsibility of overseeing financial management and ensuring fiscal responsibility for the city. This involves monitoring the city's financial activities, managing resources efficiently, and making strategic decisions to maintain a sound financial position.

As the chief executive of the city, the Mayor collaborates with the finance department and other relevant stakeholders to monitor and evaluate the city's financial performance. This includes regularly reviewing financial reports, analyzing revenue and expenditure trends, and identifying areas that require attention or corrective action.

In overseeing financial management, the Mayor plays a crucial role in ensuring that the city operates within its financial means and adheres to established financial policies and regulations. They work closely with the finance department to establish effective financial controls, implement best practices, and safeguard the city's financial assets.

The Mayor also provides guidance and direction in matters related to financial planning, revenue generation, and expenditure management. They work with city officials to develop long-term financial strategies, aligning them with the city's strategic goals and priorities. This may involve evaluating revenue streams, exploring opportunities for economic growth, and identifying areas where cost efficiencies can be achieved.

In addition, the Mayor works with City Council to establish fiscal policies, guidelines, and objectives that promote responsible financial management. They collaborate with Council members to develop financial plans that address the city's needs while ensuring transparency, accountability, and prudent use of public funds.

One of the key aspects of overseeing financial management is ensuring fiscal responsibility. The Mayor takes measures to ensure that the city's financial decisions are made in the best interest of Toronto's residents and businesses. This includes evaluating proposed expenditures, assessing their potential impact on the city's financial health, and considering the long-term sustainability of financial commitments.

The Mayor also actively engages in budgetary decisions, advocating for responsible spending, and evaluating the financial implications of proposed policies and initiatives. They work with City Council to make informed decisions on budget allocations, balancing the need for essential services, infrastructure investments, and other priorities within the available resources.

Additionally, the Mayor collaborates with auditors and internal control departments to conduct regular financial audits and reviews. This ensures compliance with financial regulations, identifies areas for improvement, and strengthens accountability within the city's financial management processes.

By overseeing financial management and ensuring fiscal responsibility, the Mayor plays a vital role in maintaining the financial stability and sustainability of Toronto. Their diligent oversight, strategic decision-making, and commitment to responsible financial practices contribute to the city's ability to meet its financial obligations, invest in its future, and provide essential services to its residents.

Through effective financial management, the Mayor helps build public trust, enhances the city's creditworthiness, and creates an environment that fosters economic growth and development. By promoting fiscal responsibility, the Mayor demonstrates a commitment to the long-term well-being of the city, its residents, and its future generations.

Relationship with City Council

Collaborating with City Council members to develop and implement policies

The Mayor of Toronto plays a critical role in collaborating with City Council members to develop and implement policies that shape the city's direction and address the needs of its residents. This collaborative approach ensures that policies are representative of the diverse perspectives and priorities of the Council members and reflect the interests of the community.

The Mayor actively engages with City Council members in policy development, working closely with them to identify key issues, set policy objectives, and explore potential solutions. This collaborative process may involve conducting research, seeking expert opinions, and consulting with stakeholders to gather diverse perspectives and inform policy decisions.

Through open and transparent communication, the Mayor fosters a climate of dialogue and exchange of ideas among Council members. They create opportunities for discussion, debate, and consensus-building, encouraging Council members to share their viewpoints and engage in constructive deliberations.

As policy proposals are developed, the Mayor leads the effort to build consensus and seek input from Council members. They engage in consultations, present policy options, and facilitate discussions to ensure that all Councilors have a voice in the decision-making process. The Mayor's role is to bridge divergent viewpoints, find common ground, and facilitate compromises that balance competing interests.

In addition to collaborating on policy development, the Mayor works closely with Council members to implement approved policies. This involves coordinating with relevant departments and agencies to ensure effective execution and monitoring of policy initiatives. The Mayor provides guidance and support to Council members in navigating the implementation process, addressing challenges, and adjusting strategies as needed.

The Mayor's collaborative approach extends beyond individual policies and initiatives to the broader strategic planning and vision for the city. They work with Council members to develop long-term plans, such as the city's official plan or strategic frameworks, which guide decision-making and shape the city's future. This collaborative effort ensures that the city's vision reflects the collective aspirations of City Council and the needs of Toronto's residents.

Collaborating with City Council members to develop and implement policies requires effective leadership, strong communication skills, and the ability to foster a culture of collaboration and cooperation. The Mayor's inclusive approach promotes transparency, accountability, and democratic decision-making, ultimately leading to policies that are well-informed, balanced, and responsive to the needs of the community.

By actively engaging with City Council members in policy development and implementation, the Mayor strengthens the relationship between the executive and legislative branches of the municipal government. This collaborative approach enhances the effectiveness of policy-making, encourages shared ownership of decisions, and ensures that the policies enacted reflect the diverse interests and values of Toronto's residents.

Building consensus and seeking input from Council members

Building consensus and seeking input from City Council members is a crucial responsibility of the Mayor of Toronto. As the leader of the municipal government, the Mayor strives to foster a collaborative and inclusive decision-making process that reflects the diverse perspectives and interests of Council members.

The Mayor understands the importance of building consensus among Council members to ensure that policies and decisions have broad support and are representative of the needs and aspirations of the community. They actively engage in dialogue with Council members, listen to their ideas and concerns, and create an environment where different viewpoints can be expressed and considered.

In building consensus, the Mayor facilitates discussions and encourages Council members to share their perspectives and contribute to the decision-making process. This may involve organizing workshops, forums, or committee meetings where Council members can engage in meaningful debates, provide feedback, and propose amendments. The Mayor's role is to guide these discussions, promote respectful dialogue, and help Council members find common ground.

Seeking input from Council members is an integral part of the decision-making process. The Mayor recognizes that Council members bring valuable insights and expertise to the table, and their input enriches the quality of policies and initiatives. The Mayor actively solicits feedback from Council members, inviting them to provide input during Council meetings, committee sessions, or through written submissions. By seeking their input, the Mayor ensures that decisions are well-informed and take into account the diverse perspectives of Council members.

In addition to formal meetings, the Mayor engages in informal conversations with Council members, fostering relationships and creating opportunities for open dialogue. These informal interactions help build trust and understanding, allowing the Mayor to better understand the concerns and priorities of individual Council members and incorporate their input into the decision-making process.

The Mayor also plays a vital role in balancing the interests of different Council members and finding common ground. They act as a mediator, working to bridge gaps, address conflicts, and facilitate compromises when necessary. The Mayor's leadership and ability to navigate differing opinions contribute to the overall effectiveness and unity of City Council.

By building consensus and seeking input from Council members, the Mayor promotes a culture of collaboration, inclusivity, and shared decision-making within the municipal government. This approach ensures that the voices of Council members are heard, that decisions are well-informed, and that the needs of the community are adequately addressed.

Ultimately, the Mayor's commitment to building consensus and seeking input enhances the legitimacy of the decision-making process, fosters a sense of ownership among Council members, and strengthens the overall governance of Toronto. It reinforces the democratic principles upon which the municipal government is built and contributes to the creation of policies and initiatives that are representative of the diverse needs and interests of the city's residents.

Presiding over Council meetings and facilitating discussions

Presiding over Council meetings and facilitating discussions is a crucial responsibility of the Mayor of Toronto. As the leader of the municipal government, the Mayor ensures that Council meetings are conducted in an orderly and productive manner, allowing for meaningful discussions and effective decision-making.

The Mayor's role as the presiding officer of Council meetings involves setting the agenda, establishing meeting protocols, and maintaining decorum throughout the proceedings. They work closely with the City Clerk's office to develop meeting agendas that encompass important matters, ensuring that the agenda reflects the needs and priorities of the city.

During Council meetings, the Mayor guides the flow of discussions, ensuring that all Council members have an opportunity to express their viewpoints and participate in the decision-making process. They enforce the rules of procedure, manage speaking times, and facilitate respectful exchanges among Council members.

In facilitating discussions, the Mayor encourages open dialogue, active engagement, and the exchange of diverse perspectives. They promote an inclusive environment where Council members feel comfortable expressing their views, asking questions, and challenging ideas. The Mayor's impartiality and fairness in managing discussions contribute to a constructive and collaborative atmosphere within Council chambers.

The Mayor also plays a key role in managing conflicts or disagreements that may arise during Council meetings. They have the responsibility to mediate disputes, address points of contention, and help Council members find common ground. The Mayor's ability to foster consensus and build unity among Council members is essential in ensuring that decisions are made in the best interest of the city and its residents.

In addition to presiding over Council meetings, the Mayor may also chair committees or task forces established by City Council. In these roles, the Mayor facilitates discussions and decision-making within smaller groups, ensuring that committee members have the opportunity to contribute their expertise and perspectives to the matters at hand.

The Mayor's leadership during Council meetings and other committee proceedings sets the tone for effective governance and decision-making in Toronto. Their ability to navigate complex discussions, manage differing opinions, and guide the deliberative process is crucial in achieving productive outcomes and advancing the city's goals.

By presiding over Council meetings and facilitating discussions, the Mayor upholds the principles of transparency, accountability, and democratic governance. They ensure that all Council members have an equal opportunity to participate, that decisions are made in a fair and inclusive manner, and that the interests of the community are adequately represented.

The Mayor's commitment to effective meeting management and facilitation contributes to the overall efficiency and effectiveness of City Council. It allows for robust debates, informed decision-making, and the development of policies and initiatives that reflect the diverse needs and interests of Toronto's residents.

Community leadership and engagement

Engaging with residents, community organizations, and stakeholders

Engaging with residents, community organizations, and stakeholders is a vital responsibility of the Mayor of Toronto. The Mayor serves as a community leader, actively seeking input, fostering relationships, and promoting civic participation to ensure that the needs and concerns of the community are effectively addressed.

The Mayor recognizes the importance of connecting with residents and understanding their perspectives. They engage in ongoing dialogue with residents through various channels such as public meetings, town halls, community forums, and online platforms. These engagements provide opportunities for the Mayor to listen to the concerns, aspirations, and ideas of residents, ensuring that their voices are heard and considered in decision-making processes.

In addition to direct interactions, the Mayor collaborates with community organizations and stakeholders who play a vital role in shaping the city. They engage with nonprofit organizations, advocacy groups, business associations, educational institutions, and other key stakeholders to build relationships, gather insights, and explore partnerships that benefit the community.

Engaging with residents, community organizations, and stakeholders involves actively participating in community events, initiatives, and celebrations. The Mayor attends neighborhood gatherings, cultural festivals, charity fundraisers, and other community activities to connect with residents and demonstrate support for their endeavors. These engagements foster a sense of belonging, unity, and pride within the community.

The Mayor also acts as a bridge between residents and the municipal government, ensuring that their concerns and issues are effectively communicated and addressed. They act as a liaison, advocating for the needs of the community at the local, regional, and national levels. The Mayor represents the interests of Toronto residents in intergovernmental forums, engages with other levels of government, and collaborates with neighboring municipalities to address common challenges and opportunities.

Furthermore, the Mayor plays a key role in promoting civic participation and community development initiatives. They encourage residents to actively engage in local decision-making processes, empowering them to contribute their ideas, expertise, and resources to enhance the well-being of the community. The Mayor supports initiatives that promote volunteerism, citizen-led projects, and grassroots efforts to create a vibrant and inclusive city.

Engaging with residents, community organizations, and stakeholders requires effective communication, active listening, and genuine empathy. The Mayor recognizes the diversity of the community and strives to ensure that all voices are represented and included. They work to create an environment where residents feel comfortable expressing their opinions, sharing their concerns, and contributing to the betterment of the city.

By actively engaging with residents, community organizations, and stakeholders, the Mayor strengthens the relationship between the municipal government and the community it serves. This approach fosters transparency, accountability, and trust, ensuring that the decisions and actions of the municipal government are aligned with the needs and aspirations of Toronto's residents.

The Mayor's commitment to community engagement enhances the sense of belonging and civic pride among residents. It promotes a culture of collaboration, inclusivity, and active citizenship, leading to a stronger, more resilient, and thriving community.

Addressing concerns and issues raised by the public

Addressing concerns and issues raised by the public is a fundamental responsibility of the Mayor of Toronto. As a community leader, the Mayor is dedicated to ensuring that the voices and concerns of residents are heard and acted upon by the municipal government.

The Mayor acknowledges that residents may have various concerns, ranging from infrastructure and public services to social issues and quality of life. They actively listen to the concerns raised by the public through various channels, such as public meetings, community forums, social media, and direct communication. The Mayor values the input of residents and recognizes that addressing their concerns is crucial for maintaining a strong and vibrant community.

When concerns are brought forward, the Mayor takes a proactive approach to address them. They collaborate with relevant city departments and agencies to investigate and find solutions to the issues raised. The Mayor works closely with city staff to ensure that concerns are thoroughly assessed, and appropriate actions are taken to resolve them in a timely and efficient manner.

In addressing concerns, the Mayor acts as an advocate for the community, utilizing their position to raise awareness, push for change, and champion the interests of the residents. They work with City Council members, community organizations, and stakeholders to develop strategies and initiatives that address the identified issues. The Mayor recognizes the importance of collaboration and partnerships in finding sustainable solutions that benefit the community as a whole.

Additionally, the Mayor plays a crucial role in communicating the progress made in addressing concerns and issues to the public. They provide updates, share information, and maintain transparency throughout the process. The Mayor ensures that residents are informed about the steps being taken to resolve their concerns, empowering them with knowledge and instilling confidence in the municipal government's commitment to their well-being.

Furthermore, the Mayor understands the significance of preventive measures in addressing concerns before they escalate. They work to identify potential issues proactively and implement preventive strategies to mitigate their impact. The Mayor collaborates with community stakeholders, experts, and relevant city departments to develop policies, programs, and initiatives that anticipate and address emerging concerns.

Addressing concerns and issues raised by the public requires empathy, effective communication, and a strong commitment to public service. The Mayor recognizes that every concern raised represents an opportunity to improve the lives of residents and enhance the overall well-being of the community. They approach each concern with diligence, respect, and a commitment to finding sustainable solutions.

By addressing concerns and issues raised by the public, the Mayor demonstrates their dedication to serving the community and improving the quality of life for all residents. This approach fosters trust, transparency, and accountability in the municipal government and reinforces the Mayor's role as a trusted advocate and leader for the community.

The Mayor's commitment to addressing concerns ensures that the municipal government remains responsive and accountable to the needs and aspirations of Toronto's residents. It contributes to the development of a community where residents feel heard, supported, and actively engaged in shaping the future of the city.

Promoting civic participation and community development initiatives

Promoting civic participation and community development initiatives is a key responsibility of the Mayor of Toronto. The Mayor recognizes the importance of actively involving residents in the decision-making processes and empowering them to contribute to the development and betterment of their communities.

The Mayor encourages and promotes civic participation by fostering a culture of engagement, inclusivity, and collaboration. They strive to create opportunities for residents to participate in local decision-making, whether it be through public consultations, community meetings, or citizen-led initiatives. The Mayor values the diverse perspectives and expertise of the residents and believes that their active involvement enriches the governance of the city.

To promote civic participation, the Mayor works closely with City Council members, community organizations, and stakeholders to create platforms and mechanisms that enable residents to have a meaningful impact on local policies and projects. They facilitate dialogue, encourage open communication, and provide resources and support to help residents actively engage in community development initiatives.

The Mayor also supports and promotes community development initiatives that enhance the social, cultural, and economic fabric of the city. They collaborate with community organizations, nonprofit groups, and businesses to identify and support projects that address community needs, promote social cohesion, and foster sustainable growth. The Mayor recognizes that community development initiatives play a vital role in creating vibrant neighborhoods, enhancing quality of life, and fostering a sense of belonging among residents.

In addition to supporting existing initiatives, the Mayor encourages residents to initiate and lead their own community development projects. They provide guidance, resources, and recognition to individuals and groups who demonstrate a commitment to making positive changes in their neighborhoods. The Mayor celebrates and showcases successful community development initiatives, inspiring others to take action and contribute to the overall well-being of the city.

Moreover, the Mayor recognizes the importance of promoting civic education and awareness. They support programs and initiatives that educate residents about their rights, responsibilities, and the workings of the municipal government. The Mayor encourages residents to stay informed, participate in public discussions, and make informed decisions that shape the future of the city.

Promoting civic participation and community development initiatives requires effective communication, collaboration, and a commitment to empowering residents. The Mayor actively communicates with residents through various channels, including social media, newsletters, and public addresses, to keep them informed about opportunities for engagement and the progress of community development projects.

By promoting civic participation and community development initiatives, the Mayor fosters a sense of ownership, pride, and responsibility among residents. This approach strengthens the social fabric of the community, promotes social cohesion, and contributes to the overall well-being and resilience of the city.

The Mayor's commitment to promoting civic participation and community development initiatives ensures that the residents of Toronto have a meaningful voice in shaping the future of their communities. It fosters a culture of active citizenship, collaboration, and collective responsibility, making Toronto a more inclusive, engaged, and prosperous city.

City administration and staff oversight

Appointing and overseeing the work of senior city officials

Appointing and overseeing the work of senior city officials is a crucial responsibility of the Mayor of Toronto. The Mayor plays a vital role in building an effective and competent city administration by carefully selecting and appointing individuals to key positions within the municipal government.

The Mayor, in collaboration with City Council, establishes a rigorous and transparent process for the recruitment and selection of senior city officials. They consider the qualifications, experience, and expertise of candidates to ensure they possess the necessary skills and knowledge to effectively carry out their responsibilities. The Mayor values diversity and inclusivity, seeking individuals who can contribute to the representation and understanding of Toronto's diverse communities.

Once appointed, the Mayor provides clear direction and expectations to senior city officials. They establish performance objectives, goals, and key performance indicators to ensure accountability and drive excellence in public service. The Mayor sets high standards of professionalism, integrity, and ethical conduct, emphasizing the importance of serving the public interest.

The Mayor oversees the work of senior city officials by actively engaging with them, seeking regular updates on their respective areas of responsibility, and providing guidance and support as needed. They foster a collaborative working relationship, encouraging open communication and the sharing of information among city officials. The Mayor understands the value of teamwork and cooperation in achieving the city's goals and objectives.

In addition to overseeing the work of senior city officials, the Mayor is responsible for evaluating their performance. They conduct regular performance assessments, providing constructive feedback and recognition for accomplishments. The Mayor ensures that senior city officials are held accountable for their actions and outcomes, promoting a culture of continuous improvement and professional development within the city administration.

The Mayor also promotes a culture of innovation and efficiency within the city administration. They encourage senior city officials to explore new ideas, adopt best practices, and implement innovative approaches to address the city's challenges and meet the evolving needs of its residents. The Mayor supports initiatives that enhance service delivery, streamline processes, and promote the effective use of resources.

Additionally, the Mayor collaborates with senior city officials to develop and implement strategic plans and policies that align with the city's vision and priorities. They provide strategic leadership, ensuring that the actions of the city administration are in line with the goals and aspirations of Toronto's residents. The Mayor fosters a shared understanding of the city's direction and promotes a unified approach to achieving its objectives.

Through the appointment and oversight of senior city officials, the Mayor ensures the effective and efficient operation of the municipal government. They strive to create a culture of excellence, professionalism, and public service within the city administration, ultimately contributing to the delivery of high-quality services and the well-being of Toronto's residents.

The Mayor's commitment to appointing and overseeing the work of senior city officials demonstrates their dedication to building a capable and accountable city administration. It reinforces their role as a leader and manager, responsible for the effective implementation of policies and the efficient use of public resources.

Collaborating with the city manager and department heads

Collaborating with the city manager and department heads is an essential responsibility of the Mayor of Toronto. The Mayor recognizes the importance of a cohesive and efficient city administration and actively engages with key personnel to ensure effective coordination and execution of municipal initiatives and policies.

The Mayor works closely with the city manager, who serves as the chief administrative officer of the municipal government. Together, they develop a strong working relationship based on mutual trust and respect. The Mayor provides strategic direction and guidance to the city manager, ensuring alignment with the city's vision, goals, and priorities. They collaborate on the development of policies, programs, and initiatives that address the needs of Toronto's residents.

The Mayor also collaborates with department heads who oversee specific areas of municipal services and operations. They engage with department heads to gain insights into departmental activities, challenges, and opportunities. The Mayor values their expertise and input, seeking their advice on matters related to their respective areas of responsibility. They work together to identify innovative solutions, streamline processes, and enhance service delivery to meet the evolving needs of the community.

Through regular meetings, the Mayor maintains open lines of communication with the city manager and department heads. They discuss ongoing projects, review progress, and address any issues or obstacles that may arise. The Mayor encourages a culture of collaboration, fostering an environment where ideas and concerns can be freely shared, and where collective problem-solving is prioritized.

In addition to collaboration within the municipal government, the Mayor facilitates cooperation and coordination between different departments and agencies. They recognize that many issues facing the city require a multidisciplinary approach and involve the participation of various stakeholders. The Mayor acts as a bridge between different departments, facilitating communication, and promoting collaboration to ensure effective outcomes and efficient use of resources.

The Mayor's collaboration with the city manager and department heads extends beyond day-to-day operations. They work together to develop long-term strategic plans and initiatives that contribute to the overall well-being and sustainable growth of Toronto. The Mayor provides leadership and guidance, ensuring that departmental activities are aligned with the city's strategic priorities and vision for the future.

Furthermore, the Mayor advocates for the needs and interests of the city administration at higher levels of government. They collaborate with the city manager and department heads to develop and present funding requests, policy proposals, and advocacy initiatives to federal and provincial counterparts. The Mayor represents the municipal government in intergovernmental relations, promoting Toronto's interests and seeking support for initiatives that benefit the city and its residents.

Through effective collaboration with the city manager and department heads, the Mayor strengthens the city administration's capacity to deliver high-quality services, address community needs, and achieve desired outcomes. They foster a culture of teamwork, innovation, and accountability, promoting a shared sense of purpose and responsibility within the municipal government.

The Mayor's commitment to collaborating with the city manager and department heads demonstrates their dedication to effective governance and leadership. By working together, they ensure the efficient operation of the municipal government, enhance service delivery, and contribute to the overall success and well-being of the City of Toronto.

Providing direction and leadership to city employees

Providing direction and leadership to city employees is a critical responsibility of the Mayor of Toronto. The Mayor recognizes that the success of the municipal government depends on the dedication, skills, and motivation of its employees. They take an active role in setting the tone, establishing expectations, and fostering a positive and productive work environment.

The Mayor leads by example, demonstrating integrity, professionalism, and a strong work ethic. They communicate their vision for the city and the municipal government's role in achieving that vision. The Mayor inspires and motivates city employees, instilling a sense of purpose and pride in their work. They promote a culture of excellence, innovation, and continuous improvement, encouraging employees to strive for excellence in their respective roles.

The Mayor provides clear and consistent direction to city employees, ensuring that they understand their roles, responsibilities, and performance expectations. They set performance objectives and key performance indicators to measure progress and success. The Mayor emphasizes accountability and results, empowering employees to take ownership of their work and contribute to the achievement of the city's goals.

The Mayor values the contributions of city employees and fosters a supportive and inclusive work environment. They encourage open communication, collaboration, and teamwork among employees, promoting a culture of respect and cooperation. The Mayor recognizes and appreciates the diverse talents and perspectives of the workforce, seeking to leverage this diversity to drive innovation and creativity within the municipal government.

In addition to providing direction, the Mayor offers guidance and support to city employees. They are accessible and approachable, encouraging employees to seek assistance and guidance when needed. The Mayor provides mentorship and professional development opportunities, recognizing the importance of investing in the growth and well-being of employees. They promote a culture of learning and continuous development, supporting employees in their career progression and personal growth.

The Mayor also advocates for the needs and interests of city employees. They represent the workforce in discussions with City Council, advocating for fair compensation, benefits, and working conditions. The Mayor recognizes the importance of a healthy work-life balance and strives to create an environment that supports the well-being and overall quality of life of employees.

The Mayor's commitment to providing direction and leadership to city employees contributes to the overall effectiveness and efficiency of the municipal government. They create a positive and supportive work environment that attracts and retains talented individuals who are committed to public service. The Mayor's leadership fosters employee engagement, satisfaction, and productivity, ultimately benefiting the residents of Toronto through improved service delivery and responsiveness.

Furthermore, the Mayor acknowledges the importance of celebrating the achievements and contributions of city employees. They recognize outstanding performance, initiatives, and innovations, acknowledging the dedication and hard work of employees. The Mayor's recognition programs and events foster a sense of pride and accomplishment among the workforce, reinforcing the importance of their contributions to the city and its residents.

Through providing direction and leadership to city employees, the Mayor demonstrates their commitment to effective and responsible governance. They cultivate a culture of excellence, collaboration, and employee well-being, driving the municipal government toward achieving its goals and delivering high-quality services to the residents of Toronto.

Emergency management

Collaborating with emergency response agencies during crises

Collaborating with emergency response agencies during crises is a vital responsibility of the Mayor of Toronto. The Mayor recognizes that effective emergency management requires close coordination and collaboration among various organizations and stakeholders. They take a proactive approach to ensure the city is prepared to respond to emergencies and works closely with emergency response agencies to develop comprehensive emergency plans.

The Mayor establishes strong relationships with local, provincial, and federal emergency response agencies, including police, fire, paramedics, and other relevant organizations. They engage in regular communication and coordination with these agencies to exchange information, discuss preparedness measures, and plan for effective response and recovery. The Mayor fosters a collaborative environment, emphasizing the importance of interagency cooperation and coordination during emergencies.

In times of crisis, the Mayor serves as the central point of contact and coordination for emergency response efforts. They work closely with emergency response agencies to assess the situation, deploy necessary resources, and coordinate the overall response strategy. The Mayor provides guidance and direction to ensure a unified and efficient response, leveraging the expertise and capabilities of the various agencies involved.

The Mayor plays a critical role in communicating with the public during emergencies. They serve as the official spokesperson, providing timely and accurate information to keep residents informed and reassured. The Mayor collaborates with emergency response agencies to deliver consistent and coordinated messages to the public, ensuring that vital information, instructions, and updates are effectively communicated through various channels.

In collaboration with emergency response agencies, the Mayor ensures that emergency plans are regularly reviewed, updated, and tested. They participate in drills, exercises, and simulations to evaluate the city's preparedness and identify areas for improvement. The Mayor takes an active role in identifying potential risks and vulnerabilities, working with agencies to develop strategies and mitigation measures to minimize the impact of emergencies on the city and its residents.

The Mayor also advocates for resources and support from higher levels of government to enhance the city's emergency response capabilities. They engage with provincial and federal counterparts, highlighting the unique challenges and needs of Toronto and seeking assistance to strengthen the city's resilience and emergency preparedness.

Collaboration with emergency response agencies during crises enables the Mayor to effectively mobilize resources, coordinate response efforts, and safeguard the well-being of Toronto's residents. The Mayor's leadership and collaboration ensure a swift and coordinated response, minimizing the impact of emergencies and facilitating a smooth transition into the recovery phase.

Furthermore, the Mayor recognizes the importance of post-emergency recovery and reconstruction. They work with emergency response agencies, community organizations, and other stakeholders to assess the damage, prioritize recovery efforts, and coordinate resources for rebuilding. The Mayor supports initiatives that promote community resilience and fosters collaboration among different sectors to ensure a comprehensive and sustainable recovery process.

Through effective collaboration with emergency response agencies during crises, the Mayor demonstrates their commitment to the safety and well-being of Toronto's residents. They prioritize emergency preparedness, response, and recovery, working hand in hand with relevant agencies to ensure a coordinated and effective emergency management system that can effectively protect and support the city and its residents in times of crisis.

Communicating with the public during emergencies

Communicating with the public during emergencies is a crucial responsibility of the Mayor of Toronto. The Mayor understands the importance of timely and accurate information to keep residents informed, calm, and safe during times of crisis. They prioritize effective communication strategies and channels to ensure that vital information reaches the public promptly.

The Mayor takes a proactive approach to emergency communication, working closely with emergency response agencies and communication experts to develop comprehensive communication plans. They ensure that clear protocols and procedures are in place to disseminate information and instructions to the public in a timely and accessible manner. The Mayor collaborates with relevant stakeholders, including media organizations, to facilitate efficient and accurate communication during emergencies.

The Mayor serves as the official spokesperson for the city during emergencies, providing regular updates, advisories, and instructions to the public. They deliver clear and concise messages, using language that is easily understood by residents of diverse backgrounds and demographics. The Mayor remains accessible and responsive to media inquiries, ensuring that accurate information is shared with the public through various media outlets.

The Mayor leverages multiple communication channels to reach a wide audience and ensure the broadest dissemination of emergency information. They utilize traditional media, such as television, radio, and print, as well as digital platforms, including social media, official websites, and mobile applications. The Mayor recognizes the importance of reaching different segments of the population and employs targeted communication strategies to ensure that vulnerable populations, non-English speakers, and individuals with disabilities receive critical information.

In collaboration with emergency response agencies, the Mayor provides updates on the evolving situation, including the status of emergency operations, evacuation procedures, shelter locations, and other relevant information. They address common concerns and provide guidance on how residents can stay safe and support the community during emergencies. The Mayor also emphasizes the importance of preparedness, urging residents to have emergency kits, evacuation plans, and stay informed about emergency protocols.

The Mayor recognizes the role of community engagement in effective emergency communication. They work with community organizations, neighborhood associations, and local leaders to ensure that information reaches all corners of the city. The Mayor encourages community members to serve as ambassadors, disseminating information within their networks and providing feedback on the effectiveness of communication efforts.

Additionally, the Mayor acknowledges the importance of two-way communication during emergencies. They establish mechanisms for residents to ask questions, seek clarification, and report emergency-related issues. The Mayor actively listens to feedback and concerns from the public, ensuring that their voices are heard and their needs are addressed. They collaborate with relevant agencies to address public inquiries promptly and transparently.

The Mayor's commitment to effective communication during emergencies instills confidence in the public and enhances the overall response and recovery efforts. By providing accurate and timely information, the Mayor enables residents to make informed decisions and take appropriate actions to protect themselves and their families. Effective communication fosters trust, reduces panic, and promotes a sense of unity and resilience within the community.

Furthermore, the Mayor recognizes the importance of post-emergency communication and recovery messaging. They work closely with communication experts and community leaders to develop post-emergency communication strategies that focus on recovery efforts, resource availability, and long-term support. The Mayor ensures that the public remains informed throughout the recovery process, providing updates on progress, available services, and community initiatives.

Through effective communication with the public during emergencies, the Mayor demonstrates their commitment to transparency, accountability, and the well-being of Toronto's residents. They prioritize clear, accessible, and timely information dissemination, empowering residents to make informed decisions and actively participate in emergency response efforts.

Ensuring the city's emergency plans are up to date

Ensuring the city's emergency plans are up to date is a critical responsibility of the Mayor of Toronto. The Mayor recognizes the dynamic nature of emergencies and the need for comprehensive, adaptable plans to effectively respond to a wide range of potential crises. They prioritize the regular review, update, and enhancement of the city's emergency plans to ensure their relevance and effectiveness.

The Mayor collaborates with emergency management experts, city officials, and relevant stakeholders to assess the city's emergency preparedness capabilities. They oversee the evaluation of existing emergency plans, identifying strengths, weaknesses, and areas for improvement. The Mayor ensures that lessons learned from past emergencies and best practices from other jurisdictions are incorporated into the city's plans, enhancing their effectiveness and responsiveness.

The Mayor works closely with emergency response agencies, community organizations, and subject matter experts to gather input and insights for plan updates. They facilitate collaborative discussions and exercises to identify emerging risks, anticipate challenges, and develop appropriate strategies and mitigation measures. The Mayor ensures that emergency plans align with evolving threats, technological advancements, and changing community needs.

The Mayor plays an active role in the development and revision of emergency policies and protocols. They work with relevant stakeholders to establish clear guidelines, procedures, and standard operating protocols for emergency response activities. The Mayor ensures that these policies are in compliance with provincial and federal regulations and are consistent with best practices in emergency management.

In addition to the development and revision of emergency plans, the Mayor prioritizes training and exercises to test and validate the city's preparedness. They collaborate with emergency response agencies and relevant stakeholders to conduct drills, simulations, and tabletop exercises to evaluate the city's response capabilities. The Mayor actively participates in these exercises, fostering a culture of preparedness and continuous improvement.

The Mayor's commitment to keeping the city's emergency plans up to date extends to public engagement and education. They promote community awareness and involvement in emergency preparedness efforts, ensuring that residents understand their roles and responsibilities during emergencies. The Mayor encourages public participation in emergency drills, workshops, and informational campaigns, empowering residents to be active contributors to the city's resilience.

Moreover, the Mayor advocates for resources and support from higher levels of government to enhance the city's emergency management capabilities. They engage with provincial and federal counterparts to secure funding, equipment, and expertise for plan development, training, and infrastructure improvements. The Mayor emphasizes the importance of intergovernmental cooperation and coordination in building a robust and effective emergency management system.

The Mayor recognizes that preparedness is an ongoing process, and emergency plans must be reviewed and updated regularly to address emerging threats and evolving circumstances. They allocate resources and establish timelines to ensure that plan revisions are completed in a timely manner. The Mayor also encourages continuous learning and knowledge sharing among city officials, emergency response agencies, and community partners to foster a culture of resilience and adaptability.

By ensuring the city's emergency plans are up to date, the Mayor demonstrates their commitment to the safety and well-being of Toronto's residents. They prioritize proactive preparedness, leveraging expertise, engaging the community, and collaborating with stakeholders to develop robust and effective emergency plans. The Mayor's leadership in this area enhances the city's overall emergency management capabilities, ensuring a swift, coordinated, and resilient response to emergencies.

4

Conclusion

This comprehensive summary highlights the multifaceted role of the Mayor and emphasizes the importance of effective leadership, decision-making, and community engagement in governing the city of Toronto.

Recap of the authority and responsibilities of the Mayor of Toronto

The authority and responsibilities of the Mayor of Toronto encompass a wide range of roles and functions that are vital for the effective governance and leadership of the city. Throughout this outline, we have explored the various dimensions of the Mayor's role and the corresponding responsibilities they hold.

As the chief executive of the city, the Mayor holds significant authority in decision-making processes and policy development. They play a central role in setting the agenda for City Council meetings, leading and chairing those meetings, and voting on bylaws and policies. Additionally, the Mayor takes an active role in proposing and advocating for new policies and initiatives that address the needs and aspirations of Toronto's residents.

The Mayor also serves as the official spokesperson for the city, representing Toronto in intergovernmental relations and acting as the voice of the city in public events, conferences, and meetings. They bear the responsibility of effectively communicating the city's positions, priorities, and accomplishments to various stakeholders and engaging with the public to address their concerns.

Budget and financial management is another crucial responsibility of the Mayor. They are responsible for preparing and presenting the annual city budget, working closely with City Council to ensure its approval, and overseeing financial management to ensure fiscal responsibility and accountability.

Building and maintaining a strong relationship with City Council is essential for effective governance. The Mayor collaborates with Council members to develop and implement policies, seeking input and building consensus to achieve shared objectives. They also preside over Council meetings, facilitating discussions and ensuring productive decision-making processes.

The Mayor demonstrates community leadership and engagement by actively engaging with residents, community organizations, and stakeholders. They address concerns raised by the public, promote civic participation, and spearhead community development initiatives that contribute to the overall well-being of the city.

City administration and staff oversight are also within the purview of the Mayor's responsibilities. They appoint and oversee the work of senior city officials, collaborate with the city manager and department heads, and provide direction and leadership to city employees, fostering a culture of excellence and efficiency.
Given the importance of emergency management, the Mayor plays a critical role in collaborating with emergency response agencies during crises, communicating with the public, and ensuring that the city's emergency plans are up to date. They work to keep residents informed, calm, and safe during emergencies, and prioritize effective communication strategies to reach a wide audience.

In conclusion, the Mayor of Toronto holds significant authority and carries diverse responsibilities that encompass policy and decision-making, representing the city, budget and financial management, relationship-building with City Council, community leadership and engagement, city administration and staff oversight, and emergency management. Through their leadership, the Mayor contributes to the prosperity, resilience, and well-being of Toronto and its residents.

Emphasis on leadership, decision-making, and community engagement

The role of the Mayor of Toronto is one of significant leadership and responsibility, requiring effective decision-making and meaningful community engagement. Throughout this outline, we have explored the diverse authority and responsibilities held by the Mayor and the impact they have on the governance and well-being of the city.

Leadership is a fundamental aspect of the Mayor's role. They provide vision, direction, and guidance to the city, setting the tone for effective governance and inspiring others to work towards shared goals. The Mayor leads by example, demonstrating integrity, transparency, and accountability in their actions and decisions. Their leadership style influences the culture and values of the municipal government, fostering an environment of trust, collaboration, and innovation.

Decision-making is a critical component of the Mayor's role. They are entrusted with making informed and responsible choices that shape the city's policies, programs, and initiatives. The Mayor must consider diverse perspectives, weigh the potential impact of decisions, and make choices that align with the best interests of Toronto and its residents. Effective decision-making requires analytical thinking, problem-solving skills, and a deep understanding of the needs and aspirations of the community.

Community engagement is paramount to successful governance. The Mayor actively engages with residents, community organizations, and stakeholders to understand their concerns, aspirations, and priorities. They foster open lines of communication, seeking input, and involving the public in decision-making processes. The Mayor recognizes the value of diverse perspectives and ensures that the voices of all Toronto residents are heard and represented.

Moreover, the Mayor advocates for inclusive and equitable policies and initiatives that address the needs of marginalized communities and promote social cohesion. They champion diversity, equity, and inclusion, working towards building a city that is fair, accessible, and inclusive for all residents.

The Mayor's emphasis on leadership, decision-making, and community engagement extends to collaboration with City Council members, city officials, and various stakeholders. They foster a collaborative and cooperative approach, seeking consensus and working towards shared objectives. The Mayor recognizes that effective governance requires the collective efforts of all stakeholders and fosters a culture of collaboration, respect, and constructive dialogue.

Additionally, the Mayor recognizes the importance of continuous learning and professional development. They stay abreast of emerging trends, best practices, and innovative approaches to governance, seeking opportunities to enhance their skills and knowledge. The Mayor actively engages in professional networks, participates in conferences and workshops, and seeks out opportunities for growth and improvement.

In conclusion, the importance of leadership, decision-making, and community engagement cannot be overstated in the role of the Mayor of Toronto. Through their leadership, the Mayor shapes the future of the city, makes responsible decisions that benefit the community, and actively engages with residents to ensure their voices are heard. The Mayor's commitment to effective governance, inclusive policies, and collaboration sets the stage for a prosperous, resilient, and vibrant Toronto.This comprehensive summary underscores the crucial role of leadership, decision-making, and community engagement in the Mayor's responsibilities. It highlights the importance of ethical and inclusive leadership, evidence-based decision-making, and active involvement of the community in shaping the city's future.

www.ingramcontent.com/pod-product-compliance
Lightning Source LLC
LaVergne TN
LVHW082359200926
848481LV00012B/3618